MENTAL MANIPULATION:

THE TOP 10 MANIPULATION TECHNIQUES

By: Ryan Scott

TABLE OF CONTENTS

Book Summary 1

PART I: Understanding Mental Manipulation **2**

Chapter 1: What is Manipulation? 3

Chapter 2: Why Learn Manipulation Techniques? 6

Chapter 3: Is Manipulation Ethical? 10

PART II: The 10 Best Manipulation Techniques **14**

#1 - The Fear-to-Relief Technique to Get Instant Results..................15

#2 - The Decoy Effect to Make People Choose Your Preferred
   Option 19

#3 - Tweak the Environment...23

#4 - Use Mirroring to Get Them to Do What You Want..................26

#5 - Overwhelm with Speed and Amount of Information to
   Process...29

#6 - Gaslighting to Distort Reality and Confuse People 33

#7 - Use Guilt to Your Advantage 36

#8 - Illusion of Choice...40

#9 - The Bribery Technique 43

#10 - Lure People in Using a Lowball Offer 46

#11 - Basic Skills to Master: Verbal & Non Verbal Communication50

BONUS: SELF DEFENSE CLASS 101 56

Conclusion... 60

BOOK SUMMARY

There are many other reasons for a person to use mental manipulation in his or her life, and effectively understanding and using them can make your life and those around you better. Think about that dream job you so desperately want. How about those office benefits that could increase your quality of life if only your boss allowed it? Perhaps you want to generate more leads in your business and reach a higher number of customers. Imagine taking control of the situations you are in, in every aspect of your life, and turning things in your own favor! Stop being second or third in line and start being first. You, too, can use mental manipulation to advance your own interests, influence change, or persuade behaviors. And it can change your life!

In this book, we will dive into the top 10 most useful manipulation techniques that will help you to put yourself and your own interests *first*. With this book, you will have all of the tools at your disposal to take your life into your own hands and come out as the winner in every situation. And guess what? Stick to the end of the book to find a few surprises and bonus chapters. Let's begin.

PART I:

UNDERSTANDING MANIPULATION

CHAPTER 1:

WHAT IS MANIPULATION?

Let's start with the basics. Before we go into the various manipulation techniques one can apply to get ahead in life, whether it's in our relationships or career, let's define what is means to manipulate another person or situation, and how we are going to go about it in this book. Manipulation, by definition, is the exertion of influence over other people for one's own advantage. It is the way we consciously and skillfully control the situation we are in, and the many factors within it.

A common misconception is that manipulation necessarily means to act in one's own interest *by gaining from others' missteps or weaknesses*. This is not strictly necessary for manipulation to take place. Both parties can gain from the manipulation techniques used by one party, as long as this person is exerting an influence on others for their personal gain. For this reason, manipulation is not necessarily considered an unethical mechanism to get ahead. In fact, many of us use manipulation throughout our daily activities without realizing it. Throughout this book, we are going to learn how to become aware of these tactics, and better manage them.

Manipulation and persuasion are seemingly used interchangeably when the exertion of influence is taking place. Although they are very similar techniques which involve influencing others, persuasion is more accurately described as aligning the influencer's objectives with their audience or customer, rather than solely looking to achieve some personal gain over others. For example, a company may use consumer behavior insights to make their services more appealing to their customers in order to provide them more value, and hence persuade them to get involved with their business. Here, the company gains from this by adding a new customer to their business. On the other end, the customer gains from obtaining a service that suits their needs better. Manipulation, on the other hand, is strictly exerting one's influence over others for *personal gain*, as explained above. Whether the other person loses, has no effect, or gains from this - it will still be referred to as manipulation.

Manipulation can be used in many contexts, and for many different purposes. In fact, it is so common in our everyday lives that we sometimes miss out on seeing its importance and power over the interactions which happen at every age, and in every domain. Let's look at some quick examples. Some people can use manipulation through physical intimidation, particularly when they are taller, stronger, or bigger than their counterpart. A child may use this tactic to get what they want at a school playground, the same way a boxer will use their physical presence to intimidate their adversary. A person may also exert influence over their romantic partner by applying the "silent treatment": a very common mechanism used to incite a desired response from another by breaking contact with them altogether.

The "guilt trip" is just as effective if not more. Often, a boss can make their employees feel guilty about mistakes made at work, before influencing them to take on more work. Perhaps a parent will use this strategy as a means to make their child understand the difference between what is considered bad and what is considered good behavior.

We have just briefly touched on some common examples of manipulation used in our everyday lives, and most likely at least one of these examples has already resonated with things you have experienced as the person being influenced, or perhaps as the exerter of influence over others. In this book, we will dive deeper into the many manipulation techniques, and provide you with all of the tools to exert or control the situations you are in. Here's why this matters to you.

CHAPTER 2:

WHY LEARN MANIPULATION TECHNIQUES?

Although this may come as a surprise to some, many people use mental manipulation for a living. Their jobs involve manipulating someone's emotional or mental state to feel or act a certain way. Think about a parent influencing their kids to act and respond in a certain way or a lawyer arguing for their client's needs. Think about a teacher in a classroom who is encouraging students to learn a certain topic. There are many other reasons for a person to use mental manipulation in his or her life, and effectively understanding and using them can make your life and those around you better. You, too, can use mental manipulation to advance your own interests, influence change, or persuade behaviors. And it can change your life!

It is true that some people have used mental manipulation at the expense of others. These people use deception and devious tactics to get their way, usually at the expense of others. They exploit and harm. For this reason, we may think of manipulation as a harmful thing. What few people know is that there is manipulation that happens all around us, and most of it is not actually harmful. There are behaviors and beliefs that are clearly harmful that you can positively influence. When you respect others around you and do not try to coerce them for devious purposes, you can employ positive, social, mental manipulation for the benefit of yourself and those around you.

Think about a promotion you want at your work, the job you are working to get, the romance you want to ignite, the friends you want to make, or any other goal you are looking to achieve. Now, depending on your motivation to accomplish these goals and the context in which you employ mental manipulation, those goals are within your grasp. And with each step you take to change your life, ask yourself if it harms yourself or others. If it does not, such as developing new friendships or receiving the promotion you are prepared for, then go for it! If it will hurt you or someone else, then maybe it is worth double-checking your timing. Sometimes waiting for a better moment to employ your mental manipulation skills is all you need to make it happen.

Part of the interesting part of mental manipulation is that you are working on changing another person. You have a goal or an objective to achieve, and you are employing tactics to encourage others to support your own objectives, even sometimes above their own. At times the goals are large and life-changing, while other times they are small and minimal. In our society, it has become taboo to consider "changing" someone else. You may often hear, "You can only control yourself." While this is true to some extent, you can have a strong influence on others. But, on the other hand, do you also hear, "find that someone that will encourage you to be the best version of yourself." Is this not contradicting the previous concept, idealizing the positive influence another person can have on your life? Relationships, after all, change you and the other person just by your presence in each other's lives. Your actions create reactions and vice versa.

It is important to note that mental manipulation is not only about serving you and your needs. For example, when you use a manipulation technique to encourage your partner to be more spontaneous, you are doing it to strengthen your relationship. You want to choose certain responses and actions to encourage his or her spontaneity, which you desire, so they are willing to choose it for you. There is no fight or disruption of your harmony. You are happy because they are more spontaneous and they are happy because you have "rewarded" this behavior in some way. It is not "bad" or "negative" to want to please your partner, to thank them for doing things for you, or for looking for ways to communicate that do not make the other feel embarrassed, belittled, or shamed. Using mental manipulation can be supportive, encouraging, and loving. It is hard to think of a more worthy reason to employ such techniques!

There are many reasons why a person chooses to use mental manipulation. Some of these reasons include:

1. You have a goal or need that you are working towards. This can be personal or professional. This can involve getting a certain job, promotion, meeting a new friend, etc.

2. You are in a leadership position and need to motivate and encourage a group of people to perform a certain way under your leadership. This is common in a sales environment when goals and quotas must be met, but in any working environment, encouraging your employees to do their tasks without reminders and to conduct their work with

enthusiasm is typically accomplished through a form of mental manipulation.

3. You are in control of an outcome, either personal or professional and need to align people and resources to achieve this outcome. This is common in a work setting where you need to meet a deadline and are reliant on others to help reach this outcome.

4. You want others around you to feel more confident and certain in their abilities. This is often seen with parents encouraging their children and supporting their healthy self-image.

5. You feel stale and stagnant in a position and need to invigorate your environment. This is referenced in the example above about influencing your partner to become more spontaneous.

6. Protecting people and their assets. For example, your elderly mother may be vulnerable to fraud and scams. You could force her to appoint you in charge of her finances, creating a rift between the two of you and making her feel like a victim, or you could manipulate her into appointing you in charge of her finances so you can ensure her assets are safe and she is cared for for the rest of her life.

CHAPTER 3:

IS MANIPULATION ETHICAL?

To many, the idea of "manipulation" and "ethics" appear to be an oxymoron. The manipulator is often seen as a lying, cheating, narcissistic person, while the person that is manipulated appears as a weak, naïve, or foolish. The degree of deceit depends on the situation, but when someone is intentionally fraudulent to get their way, at the expense of another, it can be unscrupulous. And this is how many people view and use manipulation. This is also especially true when you think about how many manipulators have to get to know their "victims" in a deep and intimate way. Manipulation is often not about casually brushing off someone unknown, but influencing people that are close and connected. It can use a person's dreams and hopes, what motivates them, and specific details about their lives to alter their behaviors.

But is changing behaviors and actions always a bad thing? As explained in the previous chapter, not always. There is a big difference between mental manipulation and exploitation. To "exploit" someone, you are intentionally using them to your own benefit, no matter how it impacts them. You deliberately act in your own interest and deny the benefit in return. This can include making someone work without profit in a slave-labor environment or taking money from an elderly person. Both actions look to make you profit financially while disregarding the fact that working conditions are poor for the workers or that the elderly person can no longer afford to pay their rent or buy groceries. It can also include emotional exploitation, meaning you could develop a relationship for personal gains, like gifts and other benefits, but not return their emotional investment or efforts. To be clear, exploiting someone for any reason is negative. It is different from mental manipulation, which is positive.

Mental manipulation is not the same as exploitation. You manipulate all day long if you think about it. You choose your clothing to project a certain image of yourself. This is a form of manipulation. You apply for a job and in the interview intentionally highlight your positive qualities while minimizing your weaknesses. This is a form of manipulation. You are developing a relationship with someone new and research more about their interests so you can find common ground or offer a topic you know they would be interested in. This is a form of manipulation. Have you been overly friendly or empathetic so you can get better service at a venue? This is a form of manipulation. You offer your kids an afternoon at the pool if they do not argue with one another through the morning. This is a form of manipulation.

You manipulate when you want to alter a person's behavior or attitude, especially when it is affecting you. And we do this because there is a gain on the other end; you get the job, you go on a second date, your kids are kind to one another. It may seem selfish to do things just so you get something in return, but this is human nature and nearly inseparable from all your thoughts and actions. Even when you are genuinely excited for another person's success, and you compliment them on a job well done, reflect on how giving this compliment to the other person feels for you. Chances are you get a warm, positive internal response. This is why you keep doing this.

Exploitation comes at another's expense. Manipulation does not have to. Both use intimate knowledge of others to get what you want. What makes manipulation positive is that it does not hurt, rather often also helps, the other person. For example, manipulating your children to not physically assault one another and finding another way to resolve their differences is a good parenting tactic! You have taught them to be better humans! And you get to be proud-as-heck of them when they treat their friends with kindness or get that job they were hoping to get. It will mainly be because it makes you look good as a parent. Does you looking good as a parent take away from your child's kindness or their many achievements? No! It is a win-win!

The same concept can be applied to research the person you are developing a relationship with. If you're interested in knowing who they are, wanting to know more about their hobbies, or passions, you make them feel good about themselves. You show them that they matter and that you care. You do not need to pretend that you are also passionate about their interests, but that you are passionate about getting to know them. Finding out why a person likes something and wanting to do things that you know they will enjoy, shows you care about who they are and what makes them happy. In return, they want to spend more time with you. This is why they agree to a second date. Does your "scoring" second date with them take away from their feelings of happiness? No! If anything, you have built a solid foundation to grow your relationship with openness and encouragement—another win-win!

Here's another example - consider a new colleague at work. You know you will be working closely with them and want to get to know them better. You put effort into asking questions and finding out what they are interested in. You want to know them intimately so you can find common ground and have a good working relationship. This will make working much better for you, but also for them. And in turn, the quality of work the two of you produce will probably be better when you get along well with one another, making work better for others in your work environment, as well. On the other hand, if you put in the effort to get to know them so you can try to get them fired and figure out how to take over their job, this is exploitation. One benefits all, while the other benefits just one: you.

Alone, mental manipulation is neither positive nor negative. This can sound contradictory to the statement earlier comparing it to exploitation, but when laid bare, the person that "wields" the manipulation determines the way it swings. It can become exploitation or it can become healthy mental manipulation. For the purpose of this book, we are going to look at how mental manipulation can be used in a positive way, and create these win-win situations we have mentioned. The tools presented here are explained and outlined for positive and supportive reasons. They are not presented to help you exploit others. The intention behind the action is different.

The burden of your ethical decisions rests on your shoulders: can you justify that your actions benefit others not just yourself?

PART II:

THE 10 BEST MANIPULATION TECHNIQUES

#1 - THE FEAR-TO-RELIEF TECHNIQUE TO GET INSTANT RESULTS

Possibly one of the most recognized forms of manipulation is the fear-to-relief technique. It uses a person's emotional response to a situation to first feel fearful or anxious and then relieved. It is a swing of emotions that can open a person up to another request to respond more positively. While it is titled "fear" to relief, a person does not need to feel fearful to then have relief. They could feel something negative first and then positive, before being lead to your request.

This is a classic "good cop, bad cop" scenario. Parenting is a good example of this in action. One parent threatens a consequence for a behavior, while the other parent swoops in as gentle and empathetic support. Then the two parents together offer a solution that the child is more likely to go with because of their rise and fall of emotional response. They may have been nervous the first "bad cop" was going to punish them, then relieved that their other parent, the "good cop," was there as a support. When both parents or just the "good cop" then asks the child to do something different, like turn off the TV and clean their room, they are more likely to do it.

The Science of Social Influence introduces an experiment with this method used in a shopping mall. A "blind" man walked up to strangers and touched them on their shoulder. At first, they are startled to be touched on the shoulder from behind, but when they see the "blind" man, they feel compassion. First, the "blind" man asked a simple question, like what the time was. Next, the friend of the "blind" man approaches to ask if they would like to purchase something or do something for them, like sign a petition or hold their bags. Those in the experiment that encountered the "blind" man, who was not actually blind, were more likely to act in accordance with the friend's request than those that did not encounter them.

Of course, this does not need to take place with only two people. This can occur when one person first threatens something, then empathizes, before asking or suggesting something. In addition, there could be several people playing the "bad cop" role, and several more playing the "good cops," before an ask is made. It depends on the situation. It is an effective method, but not the only option available to you to get the desired result. Continue reading through the other methods for mental manipulation we will cover in this book to learn other strategies.

Suggestions for effectively using the fear-to-relief method:

1. Choose an action or discussion that will cause a sense of dread, anxiety, or worry in the other person. Think of it something like, "That choice you made was not the best option. The consequence for that choice is no dessert after dinner/ going to the park/ getting a raise/ being up for a promotion/ etc."

2. If the first sentence deems it necessary, consider adding another sentence of dread for the recipient to make sure they

understand the gravity of the situation. For example, "Those choices are not supported in this environment and need to be addressed immediately."

3. Follow up with an empathetic statement. This shows the other person that you know them and you recognize that there are other influences in their decision outside of the current environment and situation. For example, an employee may have chosen to come in late again after being talked to about it, but you know that they are solely in charge of their ill mother who was recently hospitalized. You can deliver the "bad" news first to make sure they are aware that their actions are not acceptable, but follow with this compassionate statement, such as, "However, I recognize that you have a lot on your plate right now. I cannot imagine what it is like for you right now caring for your mother. I want to be able to help you, both here at the office and also at home."

4. Finish the conversation with your request. For example, you desire the employee to be on time in the future or need them to work on the weekend. Or maybe you want your child to stop throwing their toys or whining. Make sure to phrase the statement so they recognize that it is beneficial to them and you, as well as the situation. For example, "Can you please make sure to come in tomorrow by 8:30 AM instead of 9 AM to make up some of the missed time?" or "There are so many toys all over the room right now. Can you please take care of your things and carefully put them away where they belong?"

5. You can close with another positive affirmation when they

agree to your request. For example, "Thank you. I know I can count on you." Or "It is great seeing you care for your toys. It really shows how much you value them."

#2 - THE DECOY EFFECT TO MAKE PEOPLE CHOOSE YOUR PREFERRED OPTION

This strategy is very evident in retail pricing. After all, pricing is one of the most balanced parts of the marketing mix and a lot of effort is placed behind the prices set to encourage consumers to spend more money. The decoy effect is designed to encourage you to not choose the cheapest option and to select the option that is either more profitable for you or more expensive.

As an example, think about the three options presented to you. For $69, you get a five-piece set with a 900-watt engine. For $99, you get a nine-piece set and a 1,000-watt engine. For $119, you get a 12-piece set with a 1,200-watt engine. As you consider the three, you will notice that for $30 more you get a better value, with more accessories and wattage. But for just $20 more, you get all the accessories and considerably more wattage. The third choice in the middle is a viable option; however, it was placed in the middle as a decoy to move you from $69 to $119 much easier. If you face just the two options, you would possibly evaluate the value between the two, determining if the extra wattage and accessories made the purchase worth it.

When you use a decoy you create an easy way for your customers or other people to see the value in the more expensive option or your preferred option, and they will see it as a bargain. Another term used to describe the decoy effect is "asymmetric dominance effect," "attraction effect," or "asymmetrically dominated." This is what happens when someone is presented with two options and makes a certain decision, but when they are then presented with a third option, they change their decision. And they often change their decision to the original or the second option, not the decoy!

The decoy is used to make one of the other options look more favorable than it would appear alone. The perceived value is greater. People and businesses use the decoy effect to encourage people to choose another option and away from its competition. It is not a hard-sales technique but a much more subtle, mental manipulation.

This effect was first defined in the early 1980s. Three academic researchers conducted experiments on students. First, they gave them two options to choose from, the "competition", and the "target." The students made a choice and then the third option, the "decoy," was entered. The purpose of the decoy was to subtly move the student's preference from the competition to the target. They did this on a variety of topics and settings, such as alcohol, movies, and restaurants. They published the results and explained that in almost all the studies when the decoy was deployed, the likelihood of the target being selected was greatly increased.

This effect plays hand-in-hand with the "paradox of choice." People get overwhelmed when they are faced with too many choices. It dampens their ability to make a choice. To help reduce the anxiety of choosing, most people will select a few factors to help determine what they will make their decision based on. In retail settings, this is based on quantity and price. In other situations, it could be benefit and effort, etc. They select the criteria to determine which item is the best value for them. When you know what criteria a person will use to determine a "target's" value, you can develop a decoy designed with these attributes in mind, to encourage people to see the target as the informed and rational choice, rather than the other options.

Nudging is an ethical option to consider when looking to manipulate people or situations. This is because you never remove the options or the ability for the person to choose the competitor or decoy. You are simply encouraging them to see a different perspective. In social media, this effect is used to help encourage people to do different things like eat healthier, save the oceans, and use less energy. These are not negative aspirations to "nudge" people to pursue!

How to put the Decoy Effect into action:

1. Determine what price point, product, or choice you want someone to choose. This is your "target." This could be something that is much more expensive, more profitable, or more beneficial to the participants.

2. Decide on what the competition is. What is the cheaper or easier choice that people would find attractive to some extent?

3. Decide on what parameters most people will use to make a decision. This can again be on price and quantity, or it can be on location, time, effort, or other value.

4. Create a third option, your "decoy," that offers a skewed option to encourage people to select the target. This means a price point that is higher than the competitor but only a little

lower than the target, or the effort is just a little more to reach the target but a significant leap from the competition.

5. Present your three options and test to see if your "nudge" improved the odds of people selecting your target.

Stick around to learn about the remaining 8 top manipulation techniques to gain control over people and get what you want out of life. Loving this book thus-far? It would be incredible if you could share your honest opinion on this book by leaving a review at the kindle store. This can help other readers know what to expect from this book.

#3 - TWEAK THE ENVIRONMENT

One of the easiest ways to manipulate yourself and others is to tweak your environment. It is a powerful method for changing behavior. In fact, many people think that a simple alteration to your setting can be one of the easiest methods for changing behavior. Some of this includes what you put around your space, like objects, art, messages, etc. as well as what you choose not to allow in. Some people even extend this to the people that they allow in their environment.

People around you may not think those little things like this matter, but the messaging and other's behaviors are strong influences. In various studies, the results were repeated many times; it does not matter if the behavior is good or bad, the choices of others are "contagious." And the behaviors are not just about how they speak or their hobbies. A "contagious" behavior can include getting a divorce, having children, and even mental aptitude. If you want to be smart, hang out with smart people. If you want your child to be active and charitable, have them around active and charitable people and places. If you want your employees to produce results, engage them with others that have achieved them.

All the little intricacies of your physical environment are impactful as well. The temperature of a location can determine how you respond to situations. If the location is cold, your attitude is "colder." And when it is warm, you act "warmer." If you feel space is closed in and cluttered, you will feel that you are mentally closed in and cluttered. But when space feels open, airy, and clear, your mental state reflects this context. Context controls just about everything you do. If you want your family to eat healthier and smaller portions, choose smaller plates. Place the unhealthy food options further out of reach, but the healthy choices closer and more prevalent. And to bridge the gap between the context of the location and your person is your clothing. The way you choose to present yourself to others is a reflection of who you are and how you behave. It not only tells people how you act but reinforces your impression of yourself that way. If you want to see yourself as fit and healthy, wear clothing that reinforces this idea. You will see yourself that way, and tell others that this healthy lifestyle is important to you. On the other hand, if you are depressed and lonely, you will reflect this in your clothing.

There are many things you can do to control your environment to support your success and the success of others around you. If you want to motivate your team at work, put up motivational posters, have speakers come in to share motivating stories, and choose colors and accessories that subconsciously encourage motivation (like red, yellow, orange, etc.). If you want your children to sleep, remove bright art and objects and opt for more subtle colors like blues, greens, and neutral colors. Change out the light bulbs to be a lower wattage. Put up images of the moon, stars, sleeping animals, etc. All these little changes can subconsciously encourage sleep and relaxation.

The hard thing about human nature is that we are designed to do what is easiest. This means that even when you enjoy something, you are not apt to do it if it is not easy. You will be more likely to do something else that is easier, even though you do not enjoy it as much. Think of it like going for a bike ride. You love riding your bike on the scenic biking trail that is along a rambling, cool river. It is relaxing and calming for you. However, in the evening when you get home, you find yourself sitting on the couch watching the same movies over and over again. You do not enjoy it nearly as much. So why do you do it all the time and not jump on your bike? It is because your couch and familiar movies are much easier for you than getting on your bike and going along the trail. This is true for just about any situation in your life and for almost all human beings.

Making a small tweak to your environment can lead to drastic changes. Below are some suggestions on how you can make alterations to a setting to get your results:

1. Determine what action or result you want to achieve. For example, motivate your employees at work, calm your children down at night, lose weight, make more money, etc. Figure out what you want to manipulate.

2. Decide what environmental impacts this result in the most. For some, it is obvious that changing your work environment is the necessary place to start, while in other situations you will want to think about all locations to find the best place to alter.

3. Look up different subconscious messages that lead to your result. This includes colors, quotes, people, objects, design, etc. Music is another powerful influence to add or remove from your environment.

4. Begin making as many changes as are practical to support your goals. Adjust and tweak as needed. The more dramatic the change, the more dramatic the results.

#4 - USE MIRRORING TO GET THEM TO DO WHAT YOU WANT

Mirroring is a very valuable mental manipulation tool that does not require much thought or effort to accomplish. It is easy and simple. If you just finished reading the last technique, you may realize that this is a technique that most people will gravitate towards because it is easy to do! (If you did not read the last technique, this is your queue to go back to review that in a bit!)

The simple truth is that if you are good at mirroring, people will have a very hard time disliking or disagreeing with you. Throughout history, people have used their body language and mirroring to influence others in a powerful way. Even animals, such as monkeys, use mirroring in their interactions with others in their social groups. It is a natural response, but it does require attention and practice to be able to wield it effectively. You probably already mirror others subconsciously, but with a little bit more practice and attention, you can use this to manipulate others and achieve results.

The process of mirroring is simple; pose your body the same way the person you are communicating with is posed. The trick is to make it appear like you are doing it subconsciously. This means you do not want to copy the words they are saying and immediately change your body position when they do, but a shift a few seconds later or a subtle drop of the same turn of phrase or word choice can make a big difference in how you connect with the other person. The pattern of the other person's speech, the words or phrases they tend to use, the body posture, tense, pitch, tone, volume, etc. are all things to consider when mirroring another person.

The reason that this technique is so effective is that we are naturally designed to "like" things that are like us and to be wary or even afraid of things that are different. It is an instinct designed for survival. Think about most people's natural reactions to spiders, snakes, clowns, etc. All of these things are different than humans in a big way. They are unusual and our "opposite." The more different something is, the more humans generally dislike it. And the more something is like you? The more you like it. This goes for language, appearance, culture, religion, etc. Mirroring makes you appear more similar to the other person, and on that instinctual level, it makes the other person like you more. It also subconsciously encourages the other person to trust you more and feel better connected to you.

How to Integrate Mirroring to Motivate Others:

1. Observe the other person's vocabulary. This includes kinesthetic, audial, and visual. For example, the person may use the phrase; "I cannot quite put my finger on it." This is a more kinesthetic response. If they say, "the sounds about right," they are more audial. "I see what you are saying," refers to someone who is using more visual vocabulary.

2. Watch the other person's body language. Look at how they position their legs or where they place their hands and arms.

Watch to see if they keep their body still while they talk or if they "talk with their hands."

3. As you frame your conversation and responses, choose phrases that align with their vocabulary. For example, instead of describing the sound of something, choose to describe how it looked, if the person seems to be more visual. Or offer how it made you feel or what it physically felt like in that situation if they are more kinesthetic. Model your physical body to take on the body language similar to the other person. If they do not talk with their hands, consider keeping your hands still while you talk as well. If they cross his or her arms or cross their ankles while sitting, model their behavior as well.

#5 - OVERWHELM WITH SPEED AND AMOUNT OF INFORMATION TO PROCESS

When you know a lot of information, you want to talk about it. Or if you want to appear like you know a lot of information, you want to talk about it like you do. Information overload is a common situation and comes at you in the form of daily conversations, as well as exposure to technology. The more information you get exposed to, the more overwhelming it can be. And when the person that is being bombarded with information needs to make a decision, they only have so much capacity to understand and process that information. This means the ability to make an informed decision is compromised. The other person is more likely to defer to your knowledge and expertise because they are not as knowledgeable or does not have the same perceived expertise as you.

This is not a new state of being. In fact, it was first defined in the 1960s and popularized in the 1970s. For a long time, people have recognized that having too much information can cause a stalemate, rather than an inspiration to learn or thrive. If a single person has to process a lot of new information, especially complex concepts, they are less likely to make an independent decision. Their "performance," or ability to decide for themselves is minimized and making them more open to suggestions from you. Today people face an overload of information all the time. There is much more information available to them at his or her fingertips. It is easily shared and more people can be reached than ever before. However, do be careful with this tactic. It can also play against you. If you are not an expert on the topic you are sharing, the other person can easily look up information for themselves. This means speed is another important factor.

The average person speaks English about 115 words per minute. Of course, some people speak more slowly and others more quickly, but on average most people fall somewhere close to 115 words per minute. If you are nervous or excited, your speech is faster. If you are tired or bored, your speech speed is slower. The region you are from also makes a big difference in your normal speech speed. If you are from the Northeast, like New York, you are probably speaking faster than 115 words per minute, but those from the Midwest will probably have a slower gait.

In addition to words per minute, you can identify an average syllable per second. Most people speak up to five syllables per second. An average word has around three syllables. People who practice their speech and speaking times can increase their speed to about 155 words per minute. This is still an audible speed but much faster than normal. Other professional speakers, like auctioneers, can speak up to 400 words per minute! This is much faster than most people care to listen to!

Of course, you do not need to speak like an auctioneer to overwhelm others with knowledge and information. Your cadence, or speed of speech, is important to inform and engage your audience. You do not want to speak too fast, or people will tune you out. They cannot keep up so they do not even bother to try. Instead, they turn to their technology to get the information at a speed that works for them. But if you are speaking too slow they get bored, do not want to wait for the rest of the sentence, and will begin to look up the information on their phone, tablet, or computer instead of trusting you as the expert.

To help you practice your speed, listen to radio hosts. Notice how their cadence changes depending on the topic and the mood of the conversation. Their tone and speed change to keep their listeners engaged. They cannot rely on visuals, so they use their speech to hook people and keep them hooked. Like mirroring, in the previous technique, your speech speed naturally changes depending on the situation; however, it is a good idea to practice it for the best results. If you notice or have ever been told that you talk too fast or too slow, you can use this knowledge to help you find a pace that engages the most people. This is especially important when you want to influence others.

Advice to Help You Use Speed and Information to Your Advantage:

1. Record your own voice talking about something you are passionate about. Listen to your speed and tone. Think about it from an outsider's perception. Were you engaging, fast enough to catch them but slow enough for them to grasp what you are talking about? Take notes, make adjustments, and try again until you think you found a pace and tone that fit your needs.
2. Listen to radio shows that have a lot of talking. Listen to how the hosts engage their audience with speed and tone. Make notes and inject into your own presentation skills.

3. Make a list of topics you feel like you know a lot about or topics you want people to see you as an expert about. Research some information that you can share when needed. This information should be related to people and behaviors you want to address to motivate in some way. For example, if you have an employee that does not see the value in soft closes during the sale, look up information about this and gather statistics, names, studies, etc. that you can pull out. You do not need to memorize the information, but rather a bit to be familiar with the topic, enough so that you can share this information in great detail, at the right speed, to engage them and overwhelm them. Then when you have got them in a dizzy, ask them if they see the value in the process now and get a commitment that they will now do this in their presentations from now on. Chances are you will get a lot of, "yes!"

#6 - GASLIGHTING TO DISTORT REALITY AND CONFUSE PEOPLE

Sometimes people can be overconfident in their abilities and skills. They can feel secure in uncertain situations or have a skewed perception of a situation. This is common in parenting children as well as in the workplace. To encourage people to consider a different situation or question their ability, you can use gaslighting. Part of the process of gaslighting is having the other person pause to rethink their ideas, perceptions, and knowledge. Think about a child that has just learned to swim. They are confident in their ability to paddle from the middle of the four-foot pool to the edge, and when they stand on the edge of the speeding boat in the middle of the ocean, they feel confident they can make it to the beach. Instead of allowing them to try (and most likely fail) or shaming them to make them sit down, you can try gaslighting. Make them question their skills and abilities before jumping into the ocean.

This term is often used in a negative situation, mainly thanks to the play that gave the technique its name. The play, Gas Light, produced in the late 1930s, showed a husband trying to trick his wife into going "crazy." The play was later made into a movie in 1940 and again in 1944. It is true that this technique can be used for nefarious purposes, but it can also be used to encourage people to stop and rethink their choices. You can help them see a different perspective, especially if reality is very negative. Think of a child raised in a negative situation or family setting. Helping them distort this reality so they see a more positive situation can help them become a more positive person and have a better outlook on life. This is a positive influence. If you use it to drive your wife or husband crazy by making them question her sanity, this is not a good application.

Additional examples of gaslighting include phrases that encourage "withholding". These include, "I am not listening to this anymore," or "You are just trying to confuse the situation." The intention of these statements is to decline to engage in the situation. "Countering" is another form of gaslighting. These phrases encourage the person to recall situations when they were incorrect. Examples of this include, "Remember when you made a mistake like that last time you did it?" or "You were mistaken about the last time you thought that, too, remember?" These two methods encourage the other person to pause and rethink their perceptions and motivations. It offers the other person the opportunity to reconsider how they are communicating their feelings or dealing with the situation.

Other methods include "diverting" and "blocking." When using this method you stop the person from ruminating on the situation and turning the conversation to focus on the thoughts of the other person. It helps control the conversation and also brings the other person to examine their motives for the conversation. For example, "Where did that idea come from?" or "I am not going to have this conversation again." If you are facing a situation where the other person is causing a rift in your relationship over something, encourage them to think about what is valuable to them—the event or the relationship. Sometimes the conversation is not necessary or the way it is presented can be altered so that the relationship is also preserved. This called "trivializing." The way you can make the other person stop and rethink the "battle" they are trying to pick is, "are you going to let this come in between us?"

Gaslighting also involves strategic "forgetfulness." There are times when it is best to "forget" or "deny" that certain things occurred. If someone is focused on the negative all the time, and they bring up a situation from a long time ago that they use as a "crutch" in stressful times, you can say something along the lines of, "What are you talking about?" or "Are you sure that it happened exactly like that, since it was so long ago?" You can say these things and adopt these techniques in a method that does not mock or tease the other person for their perceptions or thoughts, but do so with love and encouragement.

How to Use Gaslighting to Distort Reality and Confuse People:

1. Allow the person to speak for a moment to hear what their concerns are. Listen for the situations or behaviors that this person is stuck on or repeating.
2. Determine which tactic of gaslighting is best to apply to help the other person change their perception of reality or second-guess their knowledge.
3. Follow up after presenting a gaslighting statement or question to determine if you were successful in changing the situation.

#7 - USE GUILT TO YOUR ADVANTAGE

Have you ever heard of a "guilt trip?" Can you think of a time when you felt like you were on one? It is pretty common to feel "guilted" into doing something. Another term used to describe this is "social exchange." In American society, helping others and doing things for them is a common occurrence, and doing something with the expectation of a favor being returned is also a normal part of society. However, sometimes people forget what deeds were done for them and need to be reminded as a method for motivating them to help in return.

The premise of this is simple, you do something nice for another person. You help them with something, do something for them, or offer them something they will use or enjoy. Later, when you need something, you approach that other person and make a request. Because you had extended yourself for them in the past, they are more likely to help you and comply with your request. Many times, you do not need to remind someone or say anything. People often remember the good deeds others do for them and want to "return the favor." But other times you need to ask them to "return the favor."

The best way to use this method is to "stock up" on good deeds for different people. You can do a variety of nice things or helpful things for them. You can help them move to a new house, drive them to the store, save their life, pay a bill, buy them dinner, etc. There is no shortage of good deeds that you can do. Often people encourage you to do these deeds so other people do not know it came from you, but to use this method effectively, you will want to make sure they know that you are going out of your way to being helpful to them. The more you "store" for different people, the more "favors" you can "call in."

Think about it like this, if you have a co-worker that you see is struggling on a project and you know you can help them out. You step in and help, not letting your bosses know you helped, but your co-worker is aware that without you they would have missed their deadline or not been able to deliver. One day you need some extra help on a project or need a shift covered, so you call on this co-worker to help you out. Ideally, all you have to do is ask this person for help and they will remember what you had done for them. They will feel "guilted" or compelled to help you. If they do not "remember" what you did for them, then you can say, "I know this is not ideal for you, but I really need the help and am asking you to return the favor." This should be enough to get what you need in return for your help previously. If this is not stirring the other person to help, you can share details about how you previously bailed them out and explain you need that in return now. If they are still not willing to help you, you can follow up with, "I understand it is a tough request, but I thought we had each other's backs. I must have misunderstood our working relationship but will not forget it in the future. That is too bad, though. I thought we could count on each other when we needed it."

The last sentence adds to the "guilt" of the situation, acting as a final push to encourage your co-worker to comply with your request. Of course, be realistic in your request and use your favors wisely. You do not want to "guilt" people into doing your work or responsibilities all the time; to the point where you have asked way more of them than you have ever done for them. It needs to be somewhat balanced to make sure people continue to comply when you need it.

How to Prepare to Guilt For Your Advantage:

1. Determine the people in your life that you feel can help you in your future. They may be family with financial freedom, or coworkers, or friends with additional resources. Know who is in your life and what they can bring to the table to help you should you need it. If you notice that there are gaps in your needs, look to find people who have those items you are in need of and write their names down. They may be harder to help and "stock up" good deeds with, but they are still good to have on the list.

2. Look for ways to help these people as often as you can, big and small. Sometimes they do not know that they need assistance with something, and you can step in and help them with it without their request, especially if it is very beneficial to their life or security. For example, if you notice that they are struggling right now with getting all their daily "chores" done, maybe you do their dishes when you are in his or her house or pick up some groceries when you are at the store. You can also have a meal delivered to their house when you know that they are running around and not able to make dinner that night. Look for opportunities to help and

be of assistance to these people in your life, and make sure they know that these good deeds are coming from you.

3. When you need a favor or some help, consider if it is worth "guilting" someone into helping you. Decide if it is worth "cashing in" a favor to get the assistance. If it is, consider your list of people you have done nice things for and choose the best person to help you. Make sure you are strategic in who you choose when you choose them, and how often you reach out for assistance.

4. Make sure you are clear about your needs and ask the person to comply with your needs, and remind them of all the great things you have done for them in the past.

#8 - ILLUSION OF CHOICE

You already know about the illusion of choice, even if you have never heard of the phrase before. This is because it is a common and simple mental manipulation technique that is often employed to get you to "want" to do something. Think about when you were a child. Your parent's asked what you wanted to do today, go to the library or go to the grocery store. You get to choose how to spend your afternoon. You most likely would choose to go to the library, even if you do not usually enjoy spending a long time there. You are more likely to enjoy it this time; however, because you got to choose it. You are not forced to go there and are less likely to be upset or fight against going because you selected this option for yourself. When you get older your parent's ask if you have ever thought about learning to play an instrument and what instrument you would want to learn. They ask you to think about it for a few days and let them know what instrument you chose to play. You select the cello and tell your parents that is what you want to learn. They set up the lessons and buy the instrument for you based on your choice. You excel and love playing the cello. In both scenarios, you have presented a "choice" that you were in "control" over. But in reality, this was just an illusion offered to you in order to manipulate your decision-making.

Basically, human beings like to feel in control of their own lives and like to feel like they have free will to make their own decisions. If you take free will away from them, they feel like you have taken their freedom away and will become resentful or rebellious. Even if that person would have made that same decision on their own, the fact that they did not get to choose it on their own is more powerful than the choice itself. Another way to see this is when you purchase a vehicle. If you decide that you want to get a new car, you are happy when you select the "perfect: car. But what if you totaled your last vehicle and now have to purchase a new one? You probably are not nearly as happy. The outcome is the same; you get a new car. The financial burden is also probably close to the same. The biggest difference is the illusion of choice in this scenario.

To successfully deliver the illusion of choice to someone, you need to make sure you offer more than one option. One option needs to be the action you want the person to take or the choice you want them to make, and the second option should be unattractive to the other person yet still valuable to you. You do not want to be stuck if they choose the second option, despite your best manipulation, and have to either backtrack your illusion of choice or do something you do not want. This way it is not a total loss if the other person makes the second choice. It is also important that one of the choices is attractive to the other person; much more so than the alternative you present. For example, do not offer a child to go to the grocery store or the post office. Chances are the child will think both options sound equally unattractive. But if the library is slightly more exciting than the store, they are more than likely going to choose the more attractive option.

A slightly more complex version of the illusion of choice is referred to as "Buridan's Ass." In this scenario, "ass" refers to a donkey. In Buridan's scenario he theorized that if a donkey was placed equally between hay and a trough of water, the donkey would end up dying of dehydration and starvation. He had no advantage to one or the other and could not make a decision. Instead of just choosing one, it essentially chose to die because it did not choose one of the other options. This is great to use when you do not want a person to make a choice. You give them the ability to choose between two equally burdensome or advantageous situations and allow them to select neither because they are incapable of making a rational choice. Instead of getting them to choose one or the other, you make them "choose" nothing instead.

The Best Ways to Use Illusion of Choice:

1. Determine what action or choice you want the other person to select.

2. Choose how you will present the choice to the other person. You can offer it along with another choice, present an unattractive option with the chosen option, or two equally attractive offers so the person cannot make a decision at all.

3. Make sure your alternative options are still choices that you are comfortable fulfilling should the other person not be influenced by your manipulation.

4. Present your choices and allow the other person to exercise their free will an illusion of control over the decision.

#9 - THE BRIBERY TECHNIQUE

There are many forms of bribery. And bribery is very similar to guilting. When in a bribing situation, one person exchanges something valuable in return for influence or action. The person receiving the bribe would not normally offer a valuable item or influence in another situation. You are offering something with the expectation of getting something in return. This is like guilting in that you do something for someone else in order to get a favor back in return one day, but in this case it is more direct than guilting. Bribery makes it clear that "if I do this for you, you will do that for me." The bribe is given to get something in return or to change a person's behavior. For example, if someone bestowed another with a large sum of money with the condition that a person acted a certain way or made a critical decision in their favor, this is considered bribery. A bribe is often considered a financial "gift;" however, it can be physical items like a car or house, privilege, or advantage. It can also include a promise for a vote or influence in their favor.

Determining if something is a bribe versus an equitable offer is hard sometimes. This is because a tip can be considered a normal, everyday action; however, if this tip is beyond the bounds of "normal" for the other person's behavior or actions and is bestowed so the other person does something in return, like purchase something from the tipper, it is a bribe. If a company offers rebates to all their customers because they are running a promotion; that is not a bribe. If they offer a rebate for those that give a positive review on their website, this could be considered a bribe. If they offer a rebate with the intention of influencing the customer's response to higher rates, that is definitely a bribe. Tips, gifts, perks, favors, discounts, waived fees, free food or drinks, free advertising free trips, free tickets, kickbacks, private funding, donations, contributions, sponsorship, raises, additional commission, and promotion are all possible bribes.

There is a big difference between cultures on what is considered a bribe and what is considered a norm. From one country to the next the exchange of money for certain actions or influences is normal. In America, it is unacceptable to bribe voters to vote for a certain person in the election. In another country, this may be a common practice for the politicians. Tipping in the United States is a cultural norm for a person's services, but in other countries, a tip is considered a bribe and looked down upon.

The person extending the bribe to another person is often the one with the "power." They control the transaction and are openly invested in controlling or strongly influencing the outcome of something involved with that other person. Think about a time when you need your kids to be on their "best behavior." You tell them that in exchange for that behavior, you will give them ice cream. This is a bribe. Another example is telling a team member that if they hit their quota this month you will take them out to lunch to celebrate, just you and them. This is a bribe. Neither situation is necessarily a bad thing, but it is an open and clear exchange where you are obviously trying to manipulate the outcome.

It is not uncommon to be bribed and to bribe others. Most often, the one bribing has the money to be able to do it; however, money is not the only valuable currency. Some people deal in information, goods, and other influence.

To Bribe Someone Ethically:

1. Consider the action or behavior you want a person to exhibit. Determine what you would offer in return for that action or response.
2. Explain clearly that if they choose to exhibit this behavior or action what you plan to offer them.
3. Set a deadline and clear expectations of what must be met in order to receive the bribe. Make the bribe parameters clear and obvious. For example, an extra commission of $1,000 for hitting 10% above a specific sales goal in the next five days is a bribe that is clear and timely.
4. Be transparent about the incentives and bribes. If others know that you are willing to offer value to them for doing certain actions, they are more likely to "strike a deal" with you in a similar fashion. In addition, this prevents the action from appearing "sneaky." For example, offer a bribe to one of your children in front of others. Let the other children see your one child work hard to earn their "kickback." If they see how the bribe worked and the advantage the other child was awarded, they may request a similar "deal."

#10 - LURE PEOPLE IN USING A LOWBALL OFFER

So you want to get people interested and looking at you for one reason or another? One sure method of generating a lot of attention is to offer something at an incredible price, often incredibly low. Your services or products are the lowest price in your market, and definitely among your competition. This will turn some heads. Things like, BOGO's, or "buy-one-get-one," and "buy one, get one 50% off" are examples of lowball offers.

There are many reasons people consider these lowball offers as options to get people's attention. One reason is that the pricing can be a short-term strategy, allowing you to raise the prices to a "normal" level after a certain time, especially once your marketing objectives are met. Once you get enough people looking at you, you can go back to the "average" offer. Also, customers are more likely to buy more than one product or service from you. For example, if you offer a deeply discounted service, and have an add-on option to increase the cost and value of the sale, they are more likely to purchase that second (or third… or fourth!) add on because they already think you are giving them an amazing deal with the first offer. Another reason is that you can offer a bundle. Some online retailers offer a free product, which the customer only has to pay to ship, but the customer also has the option of purchasing a bundle, with the free product, and more items, plus free shipping, which is only a relatively minimal amount above the original offer's cost.

Often the best time to do a lowball offer is when you are first in a market. You want people to try a new product or service that they are not already familiar with. You want them to "take a chance" on what you offer. And you want a lot of people taking that "chance." The more you get people trying your products or services at a good price, the more positive word of mouth marketing you will receive, which is the most valuable marketing tactic there is. In addition, if you have competition, this tactic puts them on edge. You are taking business from them and they now need to defend against you somehow. If you do not have competition, you are probably scaring them off because of your amazing offers that they cannot beat.

If you do this strategy right you can quickly gather a good chunk of the market and establish yourself as the "expert" or "go-to" in your industry. You also do not need to worry about product or services becoming "stale." This means that things do not sit on a shelf for too long or go out of style before you can turn them over. You need to focus on rapid turnover and moving large quantities of whatever lowball offer you have out there. Profits are lower with lower priced products and services, so the volume needs to be there to make sense. Also, customers may only shop from you because of the deep discount. When you raise your pricing you will lose some of those shoppers.

Another consideration when throwing out a lowball offer is that some people will see you as cheap or inferior to the competition. The low price does not necessarily mean good value to shoppers anymore. They need to see that you offer something valuable at a special low price. Making it clear that this lowball offer is only for a limited time can be helpful in not only overcoming this disadvantage but also in creating urgency so people are more apt to take action in a certain time frame.

A few more examples of lowball offers include

- A new item on the menu at a restaurant is being offered at a deep discount to encourage patrons to try it.
- A new phone provider in the area is offering introductory, new customer specials that include a deep discount on package services.
- A manufacturer offers a unit for a lowball price but the replacement parts or additional necessities are marked up to cover the difference.
- An airline offers a deep discount for tickets during off times or seasons. Often additional fees are included, such as baggage and convenience fees.

How to Set a Lowball Offer:

1. Decide what lowball offer would attract the most people to you. Think of something like a BOGO or free with just the cost of shipping.
2. Determine how you plan to make a profit or make up for the lowball offer. Are you going to only offer a discount for a short time? Will you have certain add-on's at the purchase point to make up for the discount? Will you offer a bundle that is valuable to your customer but also more profitable to you?

3. Track how people respond to your lowball offer and then stick around or are upsold on more products. If you are losing a lot of people without a sale or commitment, re-approach your lowball offer to gain more traction.

#11 - BASIC SKILLS TO MASTER: VERBAL & NON VERBAL COMMUNICATION

Surprise! We have made it to number 11. We have now covered all of the most important mental manipulation techniques. However, in order to truly excel at these, it is crucial to master verbal and non verbal communication. With these skills, all of the techniques above will be much more effective and will bring you more results.

People often talk without opening their mouths or uttering a single word. In fact, what people don't say appears to be more important than what they do say. This is body language - the messages given nonverbally through tone of voice, facial expressions, and the movement of the body. Body language is an important part of communication, but most people are not aware of the message they are giving off. Being able to understand these silent clues to someone's thought can be considered an advantage in any kind of relationship. Just listening to the words being spoken can only give half the story.

Facial expressions can also give clues to what a person is thinking. Sometimes, these thoughts are related to the conversation but not always. For example, a person might appear to be bored with the conversation, but it might just be that they are tired or have other things on their mind at the moment. It is always best to look for more than one signal at a time and compare signals to the words being spoken. Some expressions are universal to all people and are quite common, such as happiness, surprise, anger, or sadness. Nonetheless, people also make smaller expressions, called micro-expressions, that may be rather difficult to detect but are perhaps more important in reading facial expressions.

The face can be a wealth of information. People's eyebrow movements can convey surprise when they are arched and raised. Lowered brows close together show anger, while the inner corners will draw up in times of sadness. The eyes also hold clues to inner thoughts, such as flying wide open in moments of surprise or staring during anger. If you notice someone has little wrinkle lines beside their eyes, also called crow's feet, it usually means they laugh a lot. The skin crinkles there when people laugh.

The mouth also needs to be observed carefully for clues. A mouth hanging open can denote fear, while a jaw suddenly dropped open usually means a surprise. When someone is happy, the corners of their mouth turn up and draw down when the person is sad. Often, people will draw their lips into a small tight pout if they are faced with something they don't like, and they will bite their lips when anxious.

Eye contact is especially important in reading body language. Eye contact is used to let other people know when someone is ready to speak, or when it is time for someone else to speak. Sometimes, people in authority positions will use eye contact to coerce participation in a lesson or a meeting. When speaking, people can use a few seconds of eye contact to make their point more forcefully.

Eye contact held a few seconds too long indicates a need to intimidate or dominate. People flirt with their eyes, showing a possible romantic interest with a warm stare, particularly if the chin is tilted slightly downward and the lips are curled up just a bit.

The hands also convey hidden messages of their own. Some are quite obvious. Have you ever seen people point their fingers at others when being aggressive or when trying to dominate the other person through a show of superiority? When people have their fists clenched, it usually means they are angry. But other lesser known hand gestures also have meaning. Someone holding their hands behind their back is trying to show confidence and superiority. Folding the hands show that the person is holding something back. Hands held with the palms up tell us that person is not a threat, while the person with their palms down is showing a desire to exert authority over others.

People will put their hand on the side of their head when they are listening to something interesting, but what few people know is that that same hand used to support the head means negative thinking or lack of interest. Both hands locked behind the head shows a desire to dominate or control someone or something, and people who put their fingertips together in a position that looks like a church steeple show confidence.

The arms and legs tell things too. Crossed arms over the chest indicate they are closed off or feel threatened and need to protect themselves. If the person speaking crosses their arms, it generally reduces their level of credibility. People who look like they are picking small bits off their clothing may not seem like much, but in fact they are likely disagreeing with the topic of conversation. When people sit with their knees clenched tightly together, they are not open to the idea being presented, whereas, crossing the legs shows a defensive stance mentally. When someone faces the speaker and sits with their legs open, they are accepting of the conversation. Lastly, holding the arms down with the hands hidden under a garment or a table edge means that person has something to hide.

Certain gestures automatically indicate a person is trying to be deceptive. When thinking about the answer to a question, the eyes dart up and to the left. The person will rub one side of their nose. They will rub one or both eyes in an attempt to block out the images they are seeing in their imagination. Someone who doubts what is being said will scratch their neck, while someone who is nervous will swing one leg or tap one foot.

Different types of touching convey different meanings. A pat on the back is a sort of hug, and people on a first date might touch each other's arms lightly to show interest. Leaning back or moving one's arm to avoid a touch by another person indicates a lack of interest. A hug that is quickly released or very weak shows a lack of interest. A bear hug means happiness to see someone.

An important method of non-verbal communication is the handshake. The handshake is used universally and conveys more meaning than any other form of unspoken communication. The handshake has been around almost since the dawn of time. Men use it as a peace symbol, to show they weren't carrying any weapons. Another theory is that the handshake was used to check for weapons hidden in shirtsleeves since the first handshakes were done by gripping the other person's forearm and not the hand. The handshake has had many meanings throughout the years. People shook hands to show friendship or agreement with another person. Deals were sealed with a handshake; a written contract was not needed. Some societies felt that the handshake was more of an equalizing gesture than bowing, touching, or tipping a hat in greeting. By the 19th Century, etiquette books described proper handshake methods, outlining the different ways to shake hands with a lady versus shaking hands with a man.

Until recently, the handshake was a male-dominated gesture. A lady would present her hand, palm down and fingers slightly curled, for a gentle touch or a brief touch by the man's lips. Men shook hands, and little boys were taught early to approach other males with their hand held out in the handshake position. The shake was to be brief but firm, not too hard and never soft in touch. The handshake should not last too long either. In the business world, the handshake was part of what made a man, and to not shake hands was considered ignorant or rude.

While the handshake still holds its proper place in the world, it has been replaced in some circles by other gestures that are similar. The "high five," where two people slap their palms together while their hands are raised high in the air, is one of these gestures. It is similar to the "low five" gestures used during the thirties and forties by some cultures. And most recently, the handshake has been replaced by the "fist pump," where two people make loose fists and bump them into each other. While this started with sports teams, it has grown to become acceptable in many other circles as an acceptable greeting.

While the spoken word is still considered to be the primary form of communication between people, the unspoken communication of body language must never be ignored. It can give great insight into the thoughts and feelings of others.

Here are a few things to note regarding verbal communication. There are many different types of verbal skills used for communication. There is the more apparent skill - the ability to speak so that others understand, and there is listening, which is equally important. There are also the underlying skills of clarifying and reflecting. If verbal communication is to be fully effective, it cannot be isolated completely from non-verbal communication. It all comes together as a whole. Verbal communication is enhanced by the speaker's facial expressions, the tone of voice, and body language.

If there is one thing to remember about communication, it is this. Effective speaking involves three important things: the words that are spoken, how those words are said, and how those words are reinforced by the speaker's non-verbal communication. All of these things will affect how the message is sent and how it is received, and they will as a result define whether your manipulation techniques over other people are effective or not.

To learn more about how to analyze people, be sure to check out my book on this exact topic, which covers this in depth. It can be found on Amazon as an ebook and paperback around the world. If you are reading this on your kindle, simply click on the following link: https://www.amazon.com/dp/B07Q5NN8NQ.

BONUS:

SELF DEFENSE CLASS 101

Just because you use mental manipulation to your advantage in an ethical manner does not mean that others will as well. In addition, you do not want to be a "pawn" in someone else's success! To help you prevent being taken advantage of, consider this chapter your self-defense course against mental manipulation.

First, you need to recognize the situation for what it is. Just because you know about manipulation tactics does not mean that you will always be the one in control of the situation or interaction. If you are engaged in a scenario where you feel like the other person is "out manipulating" you, trust your feelings. It can be hard to put your finger on the turn of control, but you can usually tap into your emotions to tell you what is going on. If you are making decisions or saying certain things because of strong, often negative emotions, such as anxiety or fear, chances are you are being manipulated. Be aware of any "threats" to remove something from your life or the situation if you do not comply with their demands. This is "withdrawal" and is a form of manipulation. It is common in both personal and professional situations and can be damaging in both situations.

Another sure-fire sign that you are in the seat of the manipulated and not the manipulator is that the other person is convincing you that their problems or needs are more urgent or greater than yours. If you suddenly feel that you need to help them with their things first and then you can get back to your agenda, you are on the other side of the coin. This person probably spouted a lot of figures and facts to you to help convince you that their needs were the most pressing. They are probably talking faster and more expressively. Remember, this is a manipulation tactic to make you feel that they are knowledgeable in this situation and the speed and information overload is going to impair your judgment.

Once you know that you are being manipulated or that someone is trying to get their way with you, you need to have a clear plan for how to deal with it. Below are some steps you can employ to help with that:

1. Learn or recall information about the person that is trying to be manipulative. Identify the leader in the group and the weakest link in the group, if you are dealing with more than one person. Be very clear to them that you feel pressured into doing or saying something that you do not want to.

2. Flip the control by asking questions to the manipulator. Probe the person to try to throw them off their game. "Do I have an opinion in the matter?" "Does this request seem fair to you?" Types of questions like these can be just enough for you to buy time to analyze the situation more.

3. Simply refuse to do what the person is requesting. This is especially important if you are still unsure about the motives and actions of the other person. If you do not know the full

scope of the situation and are still questioning your emotions or reactions, say no. You can firmly say no and decline everything the person is advancing with or you can explain that you need time to process their request and will get back to them in 48 hours. That is enough time to go home in silence, remove distractions, turn off your phone, do not check your messages, and think about the conversation. If you still feel uneasy about the request, reply and say no again.

4. Most likely the "no" will throw the manipulator off guard, but then they will regroup and attempt again. If they approach you again with a similar or the same request, but in a different way, rebuff their approach. If you have to, just walk away from the conversation in the middle of it. You do not need to continue to be in a place where someone is not respecting your decisions. Respect yourself and remove yourself from that scenario.

5. If you are incapable of walking away, be upfront with the person trying to be manipulative. Ideally, this will occur in a private place where there will not be a scene. Be honest that you feel like they are trying to control you and that you will not let that happen. If the person is a friend or co-worker, let them know that you do want to still have an amicable relationship, but only if the other person is willing to allow you the freedom to be who you are without their manipulation. It is likely that this person will not want a close relationship with you because they cannot control your thoughts and actions. This is more often than not, so be prepared for them to be bitter, angry, or uninterested in you anymore.

6. The person may alternatively be overly flattering of your strength, wisdom, courage, etc. If they are going on and on about how amazing you are or what a great job you did, especially if it was not something extraordinary and deserving of this wild praise, you need to be wary. You may want to give in to the flattery, but that will come at a steep cost of manipulation. Thank them for the compliment but return with, "but I do not feel I did enough to truly deserve those compliments."

CONCLUSION

If you've made it this far, it means you have now covered all of the key mental manipulation techniques you need in order to start controlling the situations and people around you for your own benefits and interests. We've covered the following mental manipulation techniques:

1. The Fear-to-Relief Technique to Get Instant Results
2. The Decoy Effect to Make People Choose Your Preferred Option
3. Tweak the Environment
4. Use Mirroring to Get Them to Do What You Want
5. Overwhelm with Speed and Amount of Information to Process
6. Gaslighting to Distort Reality and Confuse People
7. Use Guilt to Your Advantage
8. Illusion of Choice
9. The Bribery Technique
10. Lure People in Using a Lowball Offer

We've also spoken about how mastering verbal & non-verbal communication is key to increasing the effectiveness of these techniques. It also plays an important role in deciding when is the best time to use them in order to reach your desired outcome. We've also added an interesting bonus on how to fight off others' efforts to undermine your own interests in order to regain back control of your personal interests. Your life is in your hands now! It's time you turn your thoughts into action, and change your life for the better.

If you enjoyed this book, I would kindly request that you help me by providing me with some feedback that takes no more than 20 seconds. It can let other readers know what they can expect from this read. I appreciate your honest feedback, and it really helps me to continue producing high quality books.

All the very best,

Ryan Scott